Finding the Answer

Congrats on winning
Womens C at the
2015 Hope Tournament !

Mary Lee Kudoff

Finding the Answer

Mary Dee Kirchoff

Tellus Books
Mebane, NC

TELLUS BOOKS

Published in the United States of America
by **Tellus Books**, an imprint of Metis, LLC
http://www.metisllc.com/
tellusbooks@metisllc.com

9 8 7 6 5 4 3 2 1

First Edition
Printed in the United States of America

Library of Congress Control Number: 2009940021

Kirchoff, Mary Dee 1955 —
Finding the Answer / Mary Dee Kirchoff
– 1st **TELLUS BOOKS**

ISBN 978–0–9822715–1–3

To my children
Corrie and Emily Jolly

Belongs to
Lisa Boger

Acknowledgements

My greatest appreciation is to my husband who supported me in the process of writing this book and assisted in making it a reality. I greatly appreciate the enthusiasm and support of my friend Mary Ann Fisher, to whom I read the chapters as they were completed. I am also grateful to my friend Ann Washburn who was always eager to hear another chapter, and to her husband Kent who provided helpful comments on the first draft. Kelley Beane has kept me connected to the racquetball world and has been a cheerleader for the book. Thanks to Paulette Millichap, a publisher and a friend, for her guidance and for believing in the book. Finally, I am grateful to all my friends who read the manuscript and gave me their feedback.

Chapter 1

May 1990

It is not what you do that defines who you are; it is who you are in what you are doing that defines you.

As I waited in the corridor in my black robe, lined up with my graduating classmates, I felt a strong desire to run away. I was thirty-five and as nervous as I could ever remember being, so much so I could barely stand it. This anxiety permeated my whole body.

I understood why I felt this way. I was about to stand in front of more than 1,000 people to give a graduation speech while receiving my degree in physical therapy. Public speaking — or even writing speeches — was not something I had much experience doing. Prior to today, the few times I gave a speech I was in front of a small classroom of students. I knew that it was natural to be nervous while on the brink of such a new experience, so I told myself to concentrate on getting over these debilitating feelings and to find a new focus.

A graduation speech was not something I had anticipated but my college senior class had elected me to be the graduation speaker and I could not let them down. Just telling myself this helped to ease my mind and allowed me to stand a little taller.

I became quiet and started rehearsing my speech

one more time. It was difficult to concentrate with the hall full of chatter and excitement, but I closed my eyes and pictured myself on stage delivering the speech. After going through the speech in my mind, I told myself I had rehearsed enough and it was time to just let it go and concentrate on something else.

My thoughts drifted to my parents. My dad had suffered a stroke just two months earlier. It totally paralyzed his right side and he worked hard in therapy, enabling him to make the trip from St. Louis to Maine for today's event. Tears of pride began to trickle down my face as I thought of the tenacity that enabled my father to be there; the appreciation I felt for the loving support of both my parents soothed my nervousness.

While walking into the gym where the graduation was to take place, it dawned on me that my experiment had worked. Prior to returning to school I had made my living as a racquetball competitor and teacher. I had learned many lessons from this experience and decided it would be a wonderful experiment to see if the lessons and strategies I had used in racquetball would bring me success in studying to be a physical therapist.

Now, as I walked into the packed gym at the University of New England, I realized with absolute assurance that the experiment had been successful. This gave me confidence and a feeling of fulfillment, similar to the feeling I had after playing my best in a racquetball tournament. I loved this feeling and held on to it, finding that it decreased my nervousness and replaced my negative thoughts with wonderful ones. I was now serene, basking in the fulfillment of my experiment and my love for my parents. This placed me in the positive state I was striving for. I had practiced my speech until I felt totally comfortable with it, and, most importantly, I knew — mentally — that I was on track. Now it was time to let go of my thoughts, enjoy the moment, and let my spirit take over and lead the way.

Chapter 2

Seventeen Years Earlier: 1973

Strength comes from participation.

When I was eighteen I arrived in Burlington, Vermont, with my mom, dad, and two younger brothers to begin my freshman year at the University of Vermont.

After I had moved into my dorm room my dad announced, "It's time to eat;" but I could not bear to leave my dorm. I was so excited to be in this place where I would be released from my home nest and could fly free in the direction of my choice that I did not want to waste any time, even for a dinner with my family. I had to stay and get settled.

"I'm really not hungry. You guys go ahead. I'll stay here and explore."

My mom looked puzzled, then disappointed . . . but then she understood.

When I watched my mom come to grips with my statement I felt relieved. I did not want to hurt her feelings; I was hungry for freedom, not for food.

I felt sad to see my family go, but at the same time a wave of excitement flowed through me as I was left on my own for the first time.

Being away from my family wasn't a totally new experience as I had spent the past four summers at Camp Minne Wonka Lodge for Girls in Northern Wisconsin, a good distance from my home in St. Louis. Yet, although I was away from my family, it was not the same as being away at the university. At camp I was under the watchful eyes of my counselors and the camp owners. Still, the camp was wonderful preparation for my university experience. It allowed me to choose my activities and develop my skills to a level that I chose. I loved the challenges and the rewards of gaining camp craft skills. If a camper completed a level of expertise in camp crafts or canoeing she was allowed to go on a four to ten day trip to secluded areas of Wisconsin, Michigan, Minnesota, or even Canada. I lived for those trips.

The university was similar in that I could choose some of my classes, but I had determined that I wanted to major in physical education and minor in math, so I also had to fulfill certain requirements. The big difference was that I would be free socially and recreationally. There was no one responsible for me.

As I walked out of my room and down to the common room shared by the three dorms of Wing, Davis, and Wilkes, my feelings changed from excitement to insecurity. I really did not know what was in store for me.

I found a lounge where I could sit and just observe people coming and going and I stayed for a while.

As I was sitting, I reflected on the strange events that led me to come to the University of Vermont. I remembered the day when I was walking down the hall at John Burroughs High School in St. Louis and my headmaster stopped me. He had never spoken to me before, so I was especially surprised by his wish to speak to me then. He told me he had spoken with the University of Vermont (also known as UVM) representatives and they were hoping I would apply to their school. He mentioned that they liked my biology SAT score and suggested I look into the school.

I will never forget that meeting because it came as such a surprise, not only because the headmaster spoke to me out of the blue, but also because a college was actively seeking me out. I had been the black sheep of the family when it came to academics. My parents had warned me that they were not sure I would be accepted into this high school, where my dad and five siblings had either graduated or were currently attending. It turned out I surprised them by getting accepted, but I worked long hours to keep my grades up to passing marks.

The fact that they mentioned my biology SAT score was a miracle as well. I was happy with it, but it was 100 to 150 points lower than my siblings' scores. However, I was grateful for this unexpected suggestion from the headmaster because when I visited UVM with my dad it was love at first sight.

I was awakened from my daydreams of these events when a young man came over and introduced himself. His name was Bob, a sophomore who lived in Davis. We chatted a little about where we each came from and he let me know he was sure I would enjoy my experience at UVM. It was a brief encounter, but I was grateful for the warm welcome.

After a while I started to feel self-conscious and headed back to my room where I found my roommate Sylvia moving in. Sylvia was a sophomore majoring in nursing. She apparently knew the girls in the adjacent

15

rooms and introduced me to everyone. On one side were Margaret and Connie, and on the other were Jane and Sue. They were all sophomores except Margaret, who was a freshman and who immediately started talking to me with a huge welcoming smile on her face. She was from the area and promised to show me around.

My parents came back from dinner and, seeing that I was comfortably settled in, they said their goodbyes and went back to their hotel. They had to leave early the next day for the long drive home.

I was sad to see them go but excited by the prospect of my new life. I knew this was the best place for me but I did not know why — I just knew.

My first class was at eight o'clock the next morning, about a mile away. I loved to bike, so I slipped on my backpack and off I went. As I rounded my dorm, I was pleasantly surprised by the spectacular view of the Green Mountains of Vermont, which were layered with a light early morning mist. I allowed my soul to be filled as I absorbed the view all the way to class.

It was a full day of classes. Two of them were physical education classes: squash and racquetball. I had never played squash, so I signed up to learn. I had loved racquetball the one time I had played it with a couple of my high school friends, so I was anxious to learn more about the game, and to play again.

I enjoyed learning how to play squash, but found racquetball easier to pick up. Racquetball also appealed to me because there were longer rallies than in squash and I got a better workout. It was played on a handball court that was twenty feet wide, forty feet long, and twenty feet high. All I needed was a racquet, which was a smaller version of a tennis racquet, and a rubber ball slightly smaller than a tennis ball. The game began when I would serve the ball by standing in a service zone in the middle of the court, bounce the ball, and then hit it so it struck the front wall and landed past the line in the middle of the court. My opponent had to strike the ball before it touched the floor twice. The ball could hit any of the walls or ceiling as long as it hit the front wall before touching the floor. We would take turns hitting the ball until one of us was unable to return the ball without it bouncing twice or hitting the floor before the front wall.

I was not one to sit and observe others play; I wanted to learn while I played. My instructor was great at getting his students playing right away, so I was in luck. There were ten courts with two players to a court. We would play for ten minutes and whoever was ahead would move up a court, and whoever was behind would move down. There was a viewing area from a balcony above the court and the instructor would shout down tips. I loved how quickly everyone learned the game, allowing for a lot of rallies, a great workout, and a lot of fun. Little did I know the impact this class would have on my future.

I felt a natural high as I went through each day at UVM. I loved the mountain setting and found my academic classes interesting. I was delighted that I could participate in so many sports and even learn new ones. My life was full of activity including intramural and varsity sports, dorm events, classes, and friendships. My constant participation in all these activities, my new experiences, and even the challenges I faced, brought me tremendous personal growth. Four years flew by and, following graduation, I found myself asking what was next.

At this time I was dating a young man from Sherburne, Vermont, which was ninety minutes south of Burlington. Following graduation, in the summer of 1977, he encouraged me to find a job near his home and it was with this goal in mind that I found a summer job with the Sherburne recreation department. I was hired as the leader of activities for the children who came to the recreation center that summer. I was surrounded by glorious mountain views, enjoyed organizing daily activities, and even had the opportunity of organizing special trips such as hiking on the nearby Appalachian Trail.

Chapter 3

Life is a flow. At times you attempt to steer, and at times it is better to just let go.

I loved Vermont so much I decided it would be a wonderful area in which to settle. During my last two years at UVM (1976–1977) I had been fortunate to be hired as a coach at South Burlington High School, which was just down the road. It was an easy transition to continue working there in the fall following graduation. I supplemented this job with a math tutoring position at a private institution in South Burlington.

These two jobs did not provide me with enough activity, so I joined a nearby health and racquet club. There I met a whole new family of people who loved racquetball. I found it easy to fit into the group. I found myself being warmly encouraged to compete in tournaments around the area. My friends informed me that there was even a professional racquetball tour. Knowing how much I loved the outdoors, I thought that I could never find my profession in an indoor sport, especially one in which you are enclosed in four walls. However, I enjoyed the competition and my new racquetball friends, so I joined them in playing a few regional tournaments.

A group from the club was planning on going to

a semi–professional tournament in Montreal, which happened to be only ninety minutes away. I loved Montreal and decided to go. I trained hard for the tournament, playing or practicing just about every day.

Before I knew it, I had become totally enthralled with the game of racquetball. It appealed to everything in me. Emotionally, I found myself enjoying the game, noticing how easy it was to improve even as a beginner; physically, racquetball provided a great workout in a short amount of time; mentally, it was fascinating to use the walls to change the angles of my shots; and, socially, I liked being around the sort of people who were attracted to the game — competitive but down to earth people. On top of everything else, I thrived on the competition. I had won the Vermont State Championship after only a couple of months' training, and although my main goal was to enjoy myself, I decided that if I trained long enough and hard enough, there might be a chance to be competitive in Montreal.

I could barely sleep the night before the Montreal tournament. Since I was not sleeping well anyway, I left for Montreal early in the morning. I started out so early that I arrived at the club at 6 a.m., just as it was opening up. I checked out the draw sheet, the order of play, and confirmed that my first match would be in three hours. I decided to use the intervening time to practice and get familiar with the courts.

This was my first semi–professional racquetball tournament. It was not a tour stop, but there were professionals from the tour playing in it. I won my first two matches, and was scheduled for a semi–final match against the women's fourth-ranked player on the tour. I had just come off the court after losing this match when my Vermont friends approached me.

"Mary Dee, that was a tough match. You played well," said Sean. "Perry, the fourth-ranked male professional racquetball player, was watching you and wants to talk to you. He asked us to let you know."

My first reaction was nervousness. I felt very small and insignificant. I was not sure how to go about addressing a top ranked player. I knew, though, that I had to; it was not everyday I was asked to speak to a tour professional. So I seated myself nearby, waiting for him to get off the phone. As he walked away from the phone, I stood up and went over to introduce myself.

Perry introduced himself and then said, "You really have a lot of potential. I am conducting some junior clinics this summer and I want to invite you to attend."

I responded, "I think I may be too old for your junior camp; I'm twenty-one."

"You're kidding," Perry said. "I thought you were about sixteen — eighteen at the most. Where are you from?"

"Originally from St. Louis, but I'm living in Burlington, Vermont right now."

Perry responded, "I am also from St. Louis. I am living in California now, but St. Louis is a Mecca for racquetball. You should go back and join the St. Louis Jewish Community Center. See Phil in membership, and tell him I sent you. There are players on the pro tour as well as many nationally ranked juniors who will play with you and help you improve your game. You are good enough to compete on the tour. In fact, you can come to my junior clinics in Indiana anyway, and help me with the juniors. Maybe I can give you a few tips. You really should take this game up seriously. The first thing you need to do is to get rid of that tennis swing and shorten your stroke."

Shocked, I said the only thing I could: "Sure. I can do that. Thanks."

I could not believe what had just happened. I already had my summer planned working in a yacht club in Shelburne. I would just have to let them know I was moving back to St. Louis. What else could I do? The fourth-ranked male player in the world had just asked me to help him with junior camps and told me I had potential to be a top player. There was no choice; I would take his advice.

On the ride home from Montreal, I felt I was riding on clouds. What just happened in Montreal reminded me about what happened in choosing a university. I had not planned on going to UVM, but felt somehow guided. I had not planned to take up racquetball seriously, but now felt it was no longer a choice; I had to keep playing.

These were totally new experiences in my young adult life. Growing up, my parents or teachers had made all my decisions but recent events had changed all that. I never dreamed life would be like this. I was experiencing feelings I had never experienced before, and I loved it. I did not want these feelings to end.

When I arrived home I flopped onto my bed and fell immediately asleep from exhaustion.

It was going to be difficult to leave this area that I had loved for the past five years, but something deep inside of me said it was time for me to pack up, say goodbye to my friends and boyfriend, and head to St. Louis to see what was in store for me. Financially, the transition would be relatively easy because I could live with my parents and keep my expenses low. Emotionally I would be supported by my parents, by my oldest brother who would be home studying for his medical boards, and by my youngest brother, who was still living at home and starting eighth grade. My boyfriend and I discussed the opportunity and agreed to see each other every one to two months. So, although it was challenging to go, I could feel it was the right decision. I packed up my Ford Pinto and headed for St. Louis.

Chapter 4

Early summer: 1978

When you let go, it is amazing and exciting what comes to you.

Soon after my arrival in St. Louis I headed over to the St. Louis Jewish Community Center. I felt a tinge of excitement as I met many of the top-ranked male players on the tour and watched them practice. There were at least four male players who were in the top ten on the tour, including the number one player in the world. I quickly saw that Perry's advice was excellent and I joined the community center.

I spent my days practicing on my own, picking up matches from the top-ranked junior players as well as other excellent open players, and I took swimming breaks in between. I would be totally exhausted when I got home in the evening, but my will to win was a motivating force, so I added sprints to my training in the hope of building my speed and quickness.

By the time I left for Indiana to assist with the National Junior Camp my body was spent. I could barely move. It felt like every muscle in my body was cramped. The pain was so incapacitating that it took a week to subside. I was limited in the amount of playing I could do at the camp, but was able to help oversee the juniors. Perry and the other instructors gave intensive instructions to the junior players and I was able to glean an enormous amount of new information. So, although the camp experience wasn't exactly what I planned, I was on a high when the camp was over. A wonderful feeling of exhilaration and joy flowed through every cell of my body as I drove back home to St. Louis. I could not wait to put what I had learned into practice.

My most important lesson was not to over train. Timmy, my eldest brother, lectured me on the physiology of muscle development. He made it clear that rest is as important as exercise. When you push muscles to fatigue, they need a day or two to recover. When you train you break down the muscle and the body needs time to replenish and build it back up. If you do not give your body time to recover, the muscle breaks down quicker than it can build back and you are left with fatigue, weakness, and cramping.

I knew he was right. I had felt the punishing results of over training at the camp. I realized at that moment that the body was not a machine that I could just push and push. I needed to respect and listen to my body. Yet, I could hear a voice inside telling me not to listen to this advice. I wasn't sure where it came from, but I did know for certain that this voice was not helpful. There was a fight going on inside my head. The fight was between the part of me that wanted to win so badly that it said, "Push and keep training the same way," and another voice that was gently suggesting that I learn from my mistakes and be open to reason.

My lesson had been a drastic one: I had been unable to function for a week due to my abuse of my body, so I opted to listen to the wiser voice. I started alternating days of strength training with days of racquetball practice, and I started taking time off to allow my body to rest and recover. I noticed that I was stiff after my strength training and found that stretching not only felt good, but also gave me improved mobility. I learned that when you break down muscle in training there is a build up of scar tissue as the muscle attempts to heal. This unwanted scar tissue needs to be removed through stretching, to return the muscle to its normal flexibility. So I began to stretch every day. I could feel the difference in my body following this training plan and noticed the improvement in my play as well.

It still felt uncomfortable taking time to rest. I thought about why this was and assumed it might have been caused by the media messages I had heard growing up. "Success comes from work," they had told me. "The harder you work, the greater the success."

I changed the message for myself to "The smarter you work, the greater the success." I would use that as my motto from now on.

Soon after coming home from the camp in Indiana I received a call from the girls' athletic director at Burroughs, offering me a part–time job starting in the fall. It would be a job coaching and teaching physical education in the afternoons. It sounded like a perfect job, but then I remembered the weekend tournaments. The athletic director was very supportive of my desire to play in the tournaments and agreed to give me the needed time off. I happily accepted the job.

Again, a wonderful opportunity had just fallen into my lap.

A few weeks later, the manager of a beautiful tennis

and racquet club needed someone to teach lessons and clinics in the mornings and offered the job to me. Again I accepted.

A feeling of freedom from concern over my future enveloped me. My route seemed to be unfolding before me, and I was enjoying the scenery, the challenges, and the experiences as I floated down the path.

Chapter 5

Fall–Winter: 1978

The greatest learning comes from the toughest lessons.

The crowd was quiet as I prepared to serve the winning point. It was the tiebreaking game of the biggest match of my life to date. I was playing in my first professional racquetball tour stop, which happened to be in my hometown of St. Louis. I had made it through the qualifying round by defeating a player who had come all the way from California. I was on a stadium court, a racquetball court with three glass walls, and the stadium seats were full. Concentration gripped me. The crowd was quiet. It seemed every spectator was holding their breath . . . but then suddenly I heard someone yell "Just have fun!" Slowly it registered; it was my mom.

I tried to shake the words out of my head as I readied my serve. Somehow I could not seem to let go of her words. There was a dialogue going on in my mind that went like this: "Should I just try to have fun or should I be intense? Should I relax and just enjoy the game, or should I put pressure on myself to win?" I could take no more time thinking about it or I would be called for stalling. I had to serve.

But, for some reason, I still could not block out what my mom had said. If I won the next point I would make it to the quarterfinals. I served and it was a long rally, but I could not put the ball away. My opponent served and there was another good rally, but she came out ahead and won the match.

I was disappointed I had lost, but not upset at my mom. I was actually grateful she never put pressure on me to win. She had gone to every one of my competitions in high school, and I appreciated her enthusiasm and support.

I did wonder, though, about my mom's statement. Was it just about fun? I asked myself this question as I watched the male and female pros play the rest of the tournament.

While I watched, I observed not only the physical skills of the men and women competitors, but also their behavior on the court. In the past I had enjoyed watching matches for entertainment. I found it especially interesting to watch the personalities on the court, as well as the way they used their physical skills.

It appeared there was no real common stroke. There were as many styles as there were players. Their personalities varied as much as their strokes. Most of the players were good sports, but it was always surprising to see how angry some of them could get and how they showed it. It was even more surprising to hear how some of the professionals complained to the referees. Was it just for fun? I still did not have the answer.

Wondering who had the best stroke and what strategies were the best led me to more questions than answers. The next month was October, when the tour would go to Las Vegas. I looked forward to the trip to continue studying the ways others played the game, as much as to continue to test my skills in competition.

The night of the trip to Las Vegas was beautiful and clear. I looked out the window of the plane and saw the bright lights of Las Vegas as we landed. In my excitement I quickly retrieved my bags and headed to the hotel. Before going up to my room I peeked into the casino just off the lobby. The scene was unbelievable, like out of the movies. The room was full of tables that were crammed with people who were gambling and appeared to be thoroughly enjoying themselves. I had to get back there as soon as possible. Quickly dropping my bags in my room, I returned to the casino.

I observed all the gambling activities in the smoky room and decided to sit at the blackjack table and try my luck. I limited myself to twenty dollars and found out soon enough that it was enough money with which to have a good time. I won some hands intermixed with losses and got so caught up in the excitement that I lost track of the hour. It was close to one in the morning before I realized the time. Once I knew it was so late I went straight up to my room. I had not realized the casinos were open all night.

I had a tough time sleeping after all the stimulation, and after some fitful sleep I awoke for my qualifying match the next morning. I was not ranked high enough to make the main draw, and so headed to my assigned court for my qualifying match. There was a feeling of heaviness in my legs as I warmed up and started to play my first match. As the match continued I could not believe how poorly I was playing. I felt like I was in a cloud, or still up in the plane. I was so sluggish. The match was quickly over in two games. I lost to an unranked player.

After my match there were complaints about the

tournament set up and I was told that the directors were going to redo the tournament draw. This gave me hope that even though I had already played a match, they would put me back in the draw. I checked the draw sheets. My name was not on them anywhere. Not only was my name not there, but the match I had played was not even on the records. I checked with the director who said he was sorry but my match had counted, and I would not be in the main tournament draw.

I felt so dejected that I just sat and moped in a secluded section of the club. My anger was not directed at anyone but myself. As I reflected back to determine why I had played so poorly, I could see clearly that my play suffered from staying up too late combined with not warming up enough. I knew better than that. My anger wouldn't seem to dissipate, so I went back to my room to calm down.

In my room I vowed to prepare properly prior to every match. I never wanted to play that way again and never wanted to feel this way again. After hanging out in my room and looking at the tourist guides, I decided not to waste a trip to Las Vegas. It was time to check out Old Vegas.

The entrance into the first casino in Old Vegas was dark. The interior was all wood, with only a few windows. I started to walk through the two wooden swinging doors into the casino, wondering what lay ahead. It was like being in a time warp back to the days of the Wild West. Above were low ceilings and a very apparent lack of lights. The wooden floors were composed of uneven boards of different shades and lengths. I wondered who had walked on these floors in the days past? The aura of the old west was strong. There was something about

Old Vegas that appealed to me more than the modern casinos. I decided to walk through each old casino, playing a couple of quarters at each, and allowing the ambiance of the old west to sink into my body. It felt great to shed my sense of disappointment and replace it with the joyful feelings of independence and discovery. I found that distracting myself was a wonderful way of getting over negative emotions.

That evening a group of tournament players were talking about visiting Hoover Dam the next day and asked me to go. I was grateful for the invitation, as I was ready to explore the area some more. The next morning we drove into the desert and I was surprised to suddenly see a huge dark blue lake just before arriving at the dam. We took a tour of the dam and were amazed by its size, and by the stories about the difficulties in its construction. Between exploring Hoover Dam and the casinos, and all that I learned from playing in that one match, I now felt the trip was well worth my money and effort.

Upon returning home I immediately started to experiment with different methods for pre–match warm ups. I attempted to stretch prior to playing, but this actually made me feel stiffer. I found that if I rode a stationary bike, then stretched, I felt great. I added to my routine by performing some sprints on the court, then some practice shots from close to the front wall. I practiced my serves and some ceiling ball shots and attempted to kill the ball off ceiling shots. Killing the ball means hitting it so low and hard that when it strikes the front wall it "dies" and no opponent can return it. This routine put me into a good grove, and I felt great. I was ready to test my new routine at a tournament.

My next tour stop was in Denver. I went through

my pre-game warm up. This was especially important in Denver since the high altitude increased the pressure in the racquetballs and they were moving much faster and bouncing much higher. It would take longer to find my groove, so I was careful to take more time in my pre-game warm-ups. This new discipline paid off and I won my first game, which was the first time I won in the first round of a professional tournament. I lost in the next round, but was much happier with my play.

I also learned an important lesson in Denver. Along with the professional division, there was an open tournament for players who had not as yet made money on the tour. I played in this tournament and made it to the finals. During the finals match I had become frustrated because my opponent was getting shots on two bounces when the rules only allow one. She was also calling hinders on me, which means she was claiming that I was blocking her from getting shots, when she could not have gotten to the ball anyway. The referee sided with my opponent, requiring us to replay the points. With much frustration, I ended up losing.

After the match I had three people come up to me to tell me I had actually won. My opponent had cheated. Reflecting honestly, it became apparent that there was nothing I could do about an opponent cheating or about miscalls, but there was something I could do about my attitude. I could control my emotions and not get frustrated; and I could practice harder and concentrate even more to bring my game up so high that no amount of cheating could stop me from winning. It worked. The next time I played this opponent I beat her 15-0 in a tiebreaker — and my lesson was complete.

I continued for the rest of that season, coaching and

teaching at the high school, giving racquetball lessons, training at the community center, and playing a tour stop about once a month. I loved going to the tournaments. Each one was an adventure to a place I had never been before. I loved exploring and learning as much as I could about competition and racquetball, and thoroughly enjoyed discovering the areas where the tour events were held.

Yet, all the time there was still one question on my mind: Was it just about fun?

Chapter 6

Spring–Early Summer: 1979

Without valleys there are no peaks.

The last tournament of the season was a national tournament in Tempe, Arizona. I was entered into the singles and doubles draws. My partner in the doubles was from Connecticut, and we had totally opposite game styles: My strengths were strategy and ball control, while my partner, Sonnie, was strong and quick. We made an excellent team. There is something very different about playing doubles compared to singles. Decisions are not made by one, but by two players — and in split seconds. Each player has to be open to the other's thoughts, which makes doubles especially exciting.

I lost early in the singles, but Sonnie and I ended up winning the doubles title in the Open National Doubles Championship. It was the first national title either of us had ever won, and we were thrilled. Tasting that success made me hungry for more.

I began to study why some players seemed to win consistently and why I could not seem to get past the round of sixteen in singles. Was I as much of an athlete as my competitors? I felt I was. Did I need to get in better shape? I did not think so, since I was working on my strength, endurance, and speed and I was never tired in the matches. Was it my skills? Well, that could be it. I had good friends tell me that my stroke was not strong and needed work. Darci, one of my friends on the tour, knew of my frustration and said I could spend the summer in her apartment on the beach in San Diego, and could train there. She would introduce me to Lou, a coach of some top players, and he could help me with my game. He lived close to San Diego, and Darci was sure he would be willing to help me for a reasonable fee.

I could not believe it. This would be an adventure at a whole new level. I immediately said I would love to stay with her. I knew it would not be easy to convince my parents, but I did not know how difficult it was going to be.

"I can not pass the opportunity up," I said in a frustrated tone. "I have got to go."

"We can't let you go. We don't want you to drive out there and live there by yourself. We don't know what trouble you will find," said my mom, and then my dad.

"You are just going to have to trust me; I have to go. I can't explain why. I just know that I have to go. I hate going against you, but you will see that it will work out," I said with conviction. I actually surprised myself by standing up to my parents so firmly.

I could not let anyone stop me from heading out to California, not even my parents.

I went on: "I am grateful that I had the job at Burroughs and the job giving lessons, but I am ready to devote one–hundred percent to the game to see if I can reach the top. I need to try or I will always wonder, what would have happened if I had given it my all? I feel I am close to breaking through, but I am missing something in my game. I think that perhaps the answer is in having the help of a coach, as well as putting my full concentration on the game."

My parents did not agree, but they knew they could not stop me as I had just turned twenty three, old enough to make my own decisions. It was the first time I went against their wishes. They could feel my determination, so they decided they had to support me in going even though they wished I would not. To show their support, my father asked if he could replace my old tires with four new Michelins. I accepted and felt grateful that I would have good tires for my trip, but I was especially relieved to feel that my parents were supporting me by making this gesture.

My car packed up, I set out early in the morning for my twenty eight hour drive to San Diego. From going to school in Vermont I was used to driving long distances and loved the process. I split the trip into three legs. First I would stop in Wichita, Kansas to visit my eldest brother Timmy, who had recently married a woman I had never met. It would be a good place to rest and recharge before making the second and third legs of the trip.

I had previously driven through Missouri on trips to Kansas City but had never driven to Wichita. As I admired the green rolling hills and farmland of Missouri, I again had the wonderful feeling of freedom I so enjoyed on long trips.

The trip was not totally relaxing because, like my parents, I knew how risky it could be to drive long distances alone. I made sure I was always aware of my surroundings, only drove in the daylight or early morning, and was careful to stop in service stations that had a safe feeling about them. I had short curly brown hair and often wore a baseball cap to give the appearance of a young man while driving.

Spending time in my car gave me plenty of opportunity to reflect on my life. It was amazing that I could just pack up and head to California. I knew not everyone could do this, and I really appreciated the fact that I had the means to do so. I had worked as a coach at a nearby high school for three out of my four years at UVM, and also as a resident assistant for the dorm association. However, the funny thing was that I never felt as if I was working for the money. I wanted to be a resident assistant so I could have a single room and could help organize events, which I loved to do. I wanted to coach because I loved coaching and wanted the experience. I appreciated the money I had earned through these jobs as it allowed me to take advantage of this opportunity.

The drive to Wichita flew by. It was wonderful to see my brother so happily married and I thoroughly enjoyed his wife Elaine. Before I left she surprised me with a bag of food that would be enough for a week. I appreciated their hospitality and was especially glad to have a new sister-in-law who was so friendly.

I headed out early in the morning hoping to complete the ten hour drive to Albuquerque, New Mexico by evening. The scenery changed from flat farmland through Kansas and Oklahoma into the plains of the Texas panhandle. The plains continued into New Mexico but canyons slowly appeared in the landscape, with sheep and cattle ranches scattered throughout. It felt like I was in a dream world with constantly changing scenery.

I found a simple motor lodge near Albuquerque that appeared to be family orientated and safe. I was extremely tired from the drive and fell asleep immediately after laying down. Morning came quickly since I awoke before dawn, knowing that this was to be my longest day of driving, about twelve hours.

Driving through Arizona was very interesting with its flatlands and occasional mountains, which rose into rugged mountain ranges interspersed with valleys. Heading into California I was impressed by the heat of the desert and decided to follow the advice of my parents and turn my air conditioning off every now and then so my car would not overheat. I certainly did not want to be stranded alone in the middle of the Mojave Desert.

Never had I seen such beautiful views as when I entered into the mountain range outside of San Diego from the desert. The contrast between the lush green of the early summer San Diego hills and the dry dust of the desert was breathtaking. This stunning contrast, together with the realization that my journey was near its end, kept my adrenaline pumping until I arrived in San Diego.

The smell of the ocean was strong as I walked up the outside stairs to my friend's apartment. Darci had not yet left for Kansas for the summer, so she greeted me as I came in.

The apartment was small, but was on the beach of San Diego bay. I only had to walk across a street and between some apartments to reach a beach on the Pacific Ocean. It was quite a change for me, having spent most of my life far from the sea. The next day, Darci showed me around and introduced me to my new coach, Lou.

Although there was plenty of fun to be had in San Diego, I was there to work on my game. I had developed a strong devotion to racquetball and was committed to making it to the top of the sport. I did not know if my competitive spirit was the result of being raised with six highly competitive brothers; all I knew was that I was driven to improve and I wouldn't let anything distract me from my game. So off I went, after a day of rest, to train in Escondido with Lou. It was different having a coach. Up to this point I had disciplined myself. I now looked forward having someone else push me.

My days were spent in strength training, doing drills with Lou, and having him watch me as I played matches. I was having a difficult time understanding exactly how he wanted me to change my stroke. Lou decided to videotape me so I could see for myself. I was amazed at the difference between how I pictured my swing compared to what the tape showed I was doing. I realized right then that video was going to play an important part in sculpting my game.

When Darci left to return to her parent's home in Kansas for the summer, I was left alone in the apartment, and alone to find my way around. I found this very difficult as it was the first time I had been truly alone. I liked it, but only to a certain extent. I loved the freedom of making all my own decisions, but also felt an emptiness that I could not explain or even understand.

California was amazing for someone with an interest in racquetball and I kept busy. There were many racquetball clubs and a number of tournaments to look forward to, even during the summer. The first tournament I entered was in Los Angeles. I headed up to LA early in the morning of the tournament, enjoying the view of the ocean to the west as I drove. I had worked hard with strength training, doing drills, and playing practice matches; I felt ready and excited to see if all my training would pay off.

Chapter 7

Summer: 1979

Experience, good or bad, can always be a good experience.

"What am I going to do now?" I thought as I headed back to San Diego after forfeiting out of the tournament in Los Angeles. I had twisted my knee while playing my first match and could barely walk. It was swollen, very painful and it made driving difficult.

I was hurting mentally as well. I complained to myself that I had made the trip to California for this wonderful opportunity, and had instead injured my knee. I asked myself again, "What am I going to do now?"

I hobbled up the steps of the apartment, elevated my leg and placed ice on it. I decided it was best to just get some rest and see how it was in the morning.

In the morning it was stiff, sore, and swollen. A racquetball friend from Los Angeles called and recommended an orthopedic doctor for me to see. He even set up the appointment. It was surprising how quickly I was able to get in and see the doctor. After examining me the doctor said I would have to have an arthrogram. This is a test in which dye is shot into the joint and an x–ray is taken to determine if there is damage in the knee. They scheduled me for the next day.

It was fascinating to look up at a screen and see the inside of my knee. The test went well and I drove home to San Diego immediately afterwards. That evening I had to call the doctor because my knee and lower leg continued to swell. The swelling was getting worse. The nurse said that this happens to about ten percent of the cases. Instead of swelling going down, it keeps increasing. The nurse recommended elevation and ice.

I was anxious. I was by myself, and thought that any minute my leg was going to pop like a balloon, it was so big. I called my coach, and he said to just try to relax and keep the ice on it.

By the next day the swelling had gone down a bit. I received a call from my doctor, who said the test was negative and that he had found no injury. I was relieved.

In seventh grade I had fallen while water skiing, causing my knee to swell, and due to the pain I was unable to walk. After about six weeks on crutches my knee was better. Then I fell ice-skating and the same symptoms reoccurred. The doctor decided to operate, but when he opened my knee he did not see any damage. He told my family that I had instability in my knee because I had grown so fast that the muscles and ligaments had not caught up with the bone growth.

Now I was guessing that, again, my knee was just unstable. I decided I would try even harder to strengthen my legs, especially my knee joints, so this would not happen again.

Four weeks later I was back on the court playing. There was a tournament in Tempe, Arizona, only a seven-hour drive from San Diego, and I wanted to go. I had good fortune last time playing in Tempe, winning the National Doubles, and did not want to miss another chance to compete there. I knew I had rushed through my recovery but felt it would be all right. However, I was proven wrong in the first match.

"I will NOT let this happen again!" I screamed into the desert while driving back from Tempe. I had re–injured my knee while cutting sharply to the ball in the first game. I was so angry I kept yelling out the car window, shouting that I was going to get strong enough that this injury never recurred. I was NOT going to play again before I was ready. This was a tough lesson.

Luckily, the injury was not as bad as the first time, so it seemed like the strengthening exercises were helping. Still, I needed a lot more rehab. I had heard that swimming was a good way to strengthen your lower joints, so I joined a club where many pro racquetball players were practicing so I could study their game and swim in the pool. Along with strength training I also worked my way up to swimming a mile every other day. I was so angry with myself for my previous lack of patience that I was fully committed to rehab.

I also spent my time watching players practice and went to tournaments just to watch. I was especially interested in the different temperaments of the players. I noticed that those who were determined and confident, and who did not react when they missed shots, were more consistent in their play.

After ten weeks I was just about ready to return to competition when I received a call, out of the blue, from a racquetball club in Manchester, New Hampshire. The manager was wondering if I was interested in a job as their club professional. This meant I would teach lessons and clinics and set up leagues. The club would also sponsor me and pay my way to tournaments. If I was interested, they would pay my way to fly there to see the club and meet the managers and owners, and in this way they would also get to know me.

I said "Sure." It did not take me long because I was ready for a change. I was no longer living in the apartment because Darci had come back from Kansas and it wasn't large enough for the two of us. I was renting a bed in my coach's house, and although I got along well with his wife and loved their baby, I was sure it was an inconvenience for them.

The timing was perfect as my good friend from high school, Shelly, had come out to visit me. We were walking on the beach in San Diego when Shelly commented that she thought I was depressed. Initially, I did not understand how I could possibly be depressed, but I was open to hearing what she had to say. Shelly had known me for thirteen years and could tell that my spirits were low. I had come to California to improve my game to a point where I could make it to the top in the nation, but so far there was no evidence I had made any headway. I suppose it was getting to me. Of course my lack of progress was mostly due to my knee injury, but that did not change the fact that it seemed like I was not progressing. I still believed I could become a top player, I had just not found the answer yet. Perhaps having a job and a purpose in helping the club members with their games would give me more structure and would help lift my spirits.

About a week later I was on a flight to visit the club. It was wonderful to be back in New England and to see all the green trees and the mountains. I hadn't realized how much I missed the area.

The club was beautiful. As I walked in, I saw a round desk with the manager taking care of members as they checked in. As I looked past the desk I could see two racquetball courts with glass side walls, and sharing a front wall. To the right of the desk was a beautiful dining room and bar with a large popcorn maker and free popcorn for the patrons.

I had no doubt that working here was the right move. I agreed to the terms of employment and flew back to San Diego to pack up and head for New Hampshire. It would be a five-day drive to New Hampshire. As I was pulling out to leave on my long trip, I turned on the radio and immediately heard Willie Nelson's "On the Road Again." To say the least, it was an appropriate song:

On the road again
Goin' places that I've never been
Seein' things that I may never see again
And I can't wait to be on the road again

My spirit rose. I knew that this was more than just a coincidence. I was literally and figuratively on the road again.

Chapter 8

October: 1979

Traveling not only distances your body from home, but it distances your mind and soul so you step out of your life and are able to reflect objectively.

I noticed that there was something about driving cross-country that caused me to reflect on my life. This time I started to think about my stay in San Diego. As I passed through town heading out towards the mountains, then the desert, I knew I would miss this beautiful area. I was ready to begin the next phase of my life in New Hampshire, but appreciated the many important lessons I had learned during my stay in San Diego.

My thoughts turned to the first lesson I had learned. Every racquetball instructor has a different approach to teaching the basic racquetball strokes. I had tried several approaches, but so far none of them had worked for me. The strokes they recommended were not only complicated, but I found that attempting to reproduce them caused pain and strained my joints. For example, I had been taught to step toward the sidewall when I hit the ball; however, this method caused me to twist and strain my knee when I rotated to make the shot. I had figured out that when I stepped toward the front wall and kept my toes pointed in that direction, rather than towards the side wall, it took the torque off my knee.

With this approach I was able to play without pain or strain on my knee.

All of a sudden I realized what was going through my mind. I had figured out this change in my stroke without anyone's assistance. It was hard for me to believe that I could actually do this as I was conditioned through years of schooling — with teacher after teacher — to just listen and learn, not to figure things out for myself. Now I experienced, in a visceral way, the fact that I could think for myself and make discoveries that even others might benefit from.

It was like a switch flipped inside of my brain. I could think and develop my own ideas. I could figure out a stroke that would be easy for others to learn; a stroke that would make my shots more consistent and benefit my game, and would free me from injury.

I then started to think of my upcoming job as director of leagues and head of racquetball promotion at the club. I became more and more excited as I drove, thinking of ways I could help the club and its members. This was one of those times when the future seemed full of promise. I knew I had more personal discoveries to make, but I now had more confidence and hope, as well as an even stronger desire to be the best I could in my sport, and in my work.

My thoughts then wandered back to my stay in San Diego. I had learned that it was not fulfilling for me to live my life just for myself. The only goal I had while in San Diego was to become better at the game of racquetball. I realized now how much I had loved my previous jobs in St. Louis and Vermont, and how much I missed working with — and for — others. Perhaps that was why my friend Shelly had found me depressed. Perhaps the fact that I was only working for myself could explained the empty feeling that I had had while living in California. It was not enough for me to simply focus on myself.

The first day of driving flew by. I found myself laying out a plan for work and for training as the beautiful California and Arizona countryside went by. I stopped in Flagstaff, Arizona, and stayed at the same hotel I had stayed in on my way out to San Diego. Having already stayed there made me feel comfortable, and I slept well.

Once again I awoke early and headed off at daybreak. I started thinking of ideas for leagues and how I could set up my lesson fees. I was looking forward to the challenge of getting as many racquetball players into the club as I could, and I was excited about being a salesperson for the sport I had come to love so much. That evening, I stopped in Amarillo, Texas. My parents' home in St. Louis was my next destination.

I was exhausted when I arrived home, having driven about eighteen hundred miles in three days. My parents were very excited to see me, and I was glad to be home.

I stayed in St. Louis three days. After my goodbyes to friends and family, I packed all my belongings into my little VW diesel Rabbit and left early in the morning. I stopped in Cleveland, Ohio, to stay with my friends the Sannas, the directors of the summer camp where I had spent nine of my summers.

I became more and more excited as I drove through New York and then Massachusetts, and on into New Hampshire. Once I arrived it was as if I could not breathe; I was so happy to be there. It was fall, the colors were beautiful and the area seemed magical. It was business as usual at the club when I arrived, but I could sense the excitement of the staff and some of the members as I was introduced that evening. The manager of the club had generously offered his extra bedroom to me until I could find my own place. I followed him there the first night. He went back to the club as I settled in for the night.

I was so excited I could barely sleep. The area was beautiful and my welcome was so friendly and warm that I could not wait to get started.

Chapter 9

Recognizing one's gifts is like finding hidden treasure.

I always knew I would never forget the night I studied for my kinesiology exam as a physical education major at the University of Vermont. It had been three years ago but I remembered that night vividly as though it were yesterday. What stood out for me was that I had actually loved studying for this exam. That was a shock, as I had not known that it was possible to love to study. In addition to the theory of kinesiology, the class also covered practical applications. The professor would set up demonstrations of body movements in specific sports and the class would have to determine if the movements were natural — meaning that the body was moving in a sequence in which all the muscles and joints were working in the way they were designed. I found these exercises fascinating and the answers came easily to me.

I was drawn to this science of human movement. Now I found myself studying it again as I viewed the videotapes of me playing racquetball. Analyzing and then correcting my own stroke was easier than I had expected, and in a short time I was able to develop the racquetball stroke I had so longed for.

It was obvious; I had been playing racquetball as if I

were playing tennis. Since I had been playing tennis from the time I was five, this pattern of movement was very strong in me. Because of this, my arm and body were not working together. My arm was doing most of the work hitting the ball, while my body remained passive. I did not have to change my stroke as much as I had to find the stroke I wanted within the one I already had. It was like an artist finding a sculpture within a piece of stone by chipping away at it piece by piece, until it appeared. I was determined to lose my big arm swing. I needed to teach my body to initiate the swing, gather up potential energy like a slingshot, and then snap through using my wrist more than my arm. In this manner my arm was saved from wear and tear. The power came from my body. I found this way of swinging made my shots more consistent.

My new stroke was very compact, with little backswing, and it did not look at all impressive. Many of the players had huge windups and hit the ball extremely hard. But I had never thought that power was as important as the need to be consistent and to protect myself from injury. My new swing had these advantages because it was a more natural movement.

I was happy with my development. The new stroke was easy to teach and easy for players to pick up. I was excited about teaching them a safer way to play. Not only would it cut down on tendonitis, but it would also ensure that fewer people would be hit by the racquet. The short backswing would work well in the confines of the small court. The more lessons I gave, the more I realized that when beginners attempted to swing as hard as possible, it resulted in a more complicated stroke then needed. Their strokes were not biomechanically sound, and they looked awkward. However, when I told them to relax —

especially in their shoulders — and to hit the ball without thinking about what they were doing, their swing would be more biomechanically correct and they developed the swing I was attempting to teach. I taught them to be conscious of their natural swing. In this way I did not have to change anything; I only had to weed out their incorrect habits and make their natural swing their habit. This method accelerated their learning curve, allowing the benefits of the new stroke to be quickly assimilated. This increased the players' satisfaction and enjoyment of the game.

I also used my physical education training in setting up leagues. In school I was taught to how to set up round robins and tournament draw sheets. For some reason I loved this type of work and soon had morning and evening leagues going. I also set up club tournaments, as well as open tournaments in which players from around the area participated.

Although I loved the work, I noticed that I became very tired as a result of the physical exertion of the lessons, clinics, and games. Fortunately I was renting a room in a house that was close to the club, so I got into the habit of working all morning, going home a couple hours in the afternoon to take a nap, and then going back to work in the late afternoon and evening.

Teaching lessons and clinics not only helped the members improve and motivated them to play more often, but it also helped my game. I started to notice that when my students thought too much about specific skills like footwork or positioning, it threw off their game and they played worse. Once they mastered these basic skills they became habitual and the students no longer had to think about what they were doing; the lessons paid off and their game improved. I started telling my students this would happen; I also started reminding myself this would happen in my own game.

This made me realize that I would go through cycles while improving my game. The first part of the cycle was recognizing a weakness. While I was improving a specific skill my overall game would go downhill. Then, as I consistently practiced the skill it would become habitual. I would eventually get through this stage of the cycle, and my game would move to a higher level. After a while I would reach a plateau and the cycle would start again. I found that by acknowledging this process I could eliminate my frustration. Instead, I developed the faith that when I was in the section of the cycle in which my game went downhill (a "slump") I would get through that phase soon enough with practice. When I did, I would be a better player.

One of my weaknesses was the fact that, at times, I was tense when I competed and this decreased my control. As I experimented with ideas for correcting this weakness, I remembered my yoga breathing. My mom had consistently yelled out to me while I was playing sports in high school, "Don't forget to do your yoga breathing." Although this was somewhat embarrassing and annoying, I found that my mom was actually right. I did feel better when I did yoga breathing. Yoga breathing is breathing deeply in through your nose and out through your mouth. So, in between points, I started concentrating on just my breathing and nothing else. As I blew out my breath, I would picture my negative thoughts being blown out of my head. I found this relaxing, my stress decreased, and I played better.

When I mastered my yoga breathing, I noticed I was

playing better. Then I reached a plateau in my game and so I switched my focus to the next technique I needed to improve. I realized that instead of moving my feet, I was reaching for the ball, so I started to think about keeping my elbow closer to my body instead of reaching, and I found that this improved my game as well. I practiced this technique until I felt I had mastered it, I was again playing better but then I reached another plateau. Pretty soon I found a pattern. It wasn't that these ideas stopped working; by concentrating on a single skill, that skill became a habit. I got better, but once the skill became habitual, my growth stopped. Therefore, I had to find something else that needed work, but just one objective at a time. When I worked on only one skill at a time, it allowed me to make this skill a habit faster and more efficiently than when I was working on two objectives.

All of this work occurred in my practice matches, since tournament play required a different type of concentration. When playing practice matches I found I could concentrate on improving my game, taking certain physical skills and repeating them over and over so they became habitual. In this way I could develop skills to use in tournament play, knowing I would no longer need to think about them. When it came to playing a tournament, the more I let go of thought and just reacted, the better I played. I realized my unconscious mind was quicker and smoother in its reactions than the conscious mind.

As a child I took piano lessons for ten years and likened the process I had developed to the process of learning to play the piano. When I played a memorized piece in a recital I did not think about my finger placement, or what each note was, or whether to play it soft or loud; that is what I did in practice. When I played it in a recital or for enjoyment, I would just relax and play, and enjoy the music without thinking. Thinking actually took me out of flow of the piece. It was the same in typing. When I first learned to type, I was very slow as I had to think about every key; once I taught my conscious mind where the keys were, I could go faster. Even after I knew where the keys were, I found that if I thought about each key and what I was doing, I was much slower than if I just typed without thinking.

This helped me to realize that if I practiced the same shot over and over, I built a pathway into my body — a habit — so that I did not think but just reacted. I would immediately fall into the groove of that pathway and I would make the shot without concentrating on what I was doing. I learned to appreciate the importance of doing drills in the court by myself, and then just reacting to shots in the matches so my body would fall into the patterns I had developed in practice.

As I started working on reacting automatically in tournament play I found my mind would drift into negative thoughts like, "I am going to lose," or "That player hits harder and better than I do," or "I had better get this next point or I lose." These thoughts penetrated my body causing tightness in my skeletal muscles, which translated into mistakes such as hitting the ball into the floor, thereby losing the point. I realized I needed to block these thoughts. I found that I could train my brain by replacing these negative thoughts with positive ones. The more I practiced this technique the less often negative thoughts would come in. In this way I learned that training my mind into good habits was as important as training my body.

To fight off the negative thoughts in tournament play I found that I could say a word like "relax," or the phrase "stay on your toes," over and over again, and block the negative thoughts that hindered my game.

It did not take long for me to find the correlation between thinking negative thoughts and making bad shots. I noticed that if I gave too much attention to a bad shot by getting upset about it, I would make the same bad shot again. I saw this connection in my students as well. When my students got frustrated they would tense their muscles and their shots would be out of control. I soon discovered that blocking out negative thoughts was a real key to success.

One of my biggest lessons on blocking distracting thoughts came from Rick, one of the club members. There were so many members who wanted to play me that I would have been worn out if I played them all. I decided to play anyone who asked, but if they lost the match they would have to pay me half of a lesson fee. One day Rick decided he would distract me by taping a $100 bill on the back wall. He said that if I won, he would give me the $100. I could not stop thinking about that $100 and did not play my best. I lost the match, even though I usually beat Rick. I realized that in order to play my best I needed to keep my concentration on my game and not on the rewards.

As a result of training thirty to thirty-five hours a week, as well as playing, practicing by myself, doing aerobics and weight machines, perfecting my new stroke, and constantly studying the game, I slowly rose in the ranks on the professional tour. By the spring of the 1981 season, I was twenty-six years old and had reached my goal of making it into the top sixteen on the tour. I had played pro stops in Boise, Seattle, Chicago, and Providence.

I enjoyed the challenges of working on my game and of helping other players improve, but I still had much to learn. There was something more to discover in my game. As long as I felt I was learning and improving, I was going to keep trying to make it to the top.

Chapter 10

1982–1983

At times you make decisions, not knowing if they are good or bad. It is in the experience itself that you find that all decisions are good and bad.

It was love at first sight. I was exploring a five-acre lot, including six hundred feet of river frontage, which was for sale by one of the club members. The sound of the flowing river rippling through a narrow rocky gap before going under a bridge could be heard constantly in the background. I walked down the wooded banks of the river as it wound around the land, then up the hill to a small clearing overlooking the river. It was a perfect location for a home and I was smitten.

Now that I was in a routine at the club, I found that just playing and teaching racquetball was not fulfilling enough for me. I spent most of my life at the club and felt that I needed to be making a home, not just spending money; I wanted some sort of investment.

I was now twenty-seven and I found myself noticing how many women my age were married. I tried to figure out why I was not. I knew it was not that I was isolated from meeting available men; I met them constantly at the racquetball club. However, I was not in a serious relationship, so I decided I was not going to wait around.

I was ready to settle down and make a home, with or without someone else.

I agreed to purchase the land and have my home built. I found and hauled all the stone from my land for the mason to build my stone hearth and chimney, helped clear the land for the driveway, helped paint and do odds and ends, and gathered wood for my wood stove. I will never forget my first night in my own new home in the woods. It was New Year's Eve and I opted to skip the club's New Year's Eve party so I could celebrate the New Year with my new home and in front of my new wood stove. I had one glass of wine and went to sleep very contentedly on the floor, next to my new stove. It was great having something else in my life besides racquetball. My new home helped me keep racquetball in perspective.

My home was in Weare, New Hampshire, forty–five minutes away from my work and social life. It was my proximity to the town of North Weare that made me bear the brunt of many jokes, as my family and friends would say that I lived "nowhere" (No. Weare).

As much as I loved my home, it did not take long to realize that it was difficult to date someone when I lived forty–five minutes out in the country. A few years later I would sell my home to decrease my travel time and improve my social life. Although I found that the home did not give me the long–term fulfillment I had hoped, it was a wonderful experience and a wonderful chapter in my life.

Prior to selling my home, I had gotten more involved with the amateur racquetball association by becoming a director of amateur tournaments. The head of the New Hampshire Amateur Racquetball Association, Benny, suggested that I regain my amateur status. In this way I could play in the amateur tournaments around the area, many of them for money, and I would be eligible to play on the US National Racquetball Team. Benny went on to explain that many of the women professionals had already regained their amateur status. By keeping their amateur status they could play every weekend in amateur tournaments and still play on the professional tour. As amateurs they could keep their amateur tournament winnings, but not their professional winnings. Because there were more amateur than professional tournaments they earned a better living then the professionals. I could see the advantages. I had not made much money on the professional tour anyway, as the purses were small. My expenses had far exceeded my earnings. The thought of making the US Team and representing my country made me even more enthusiastic about playing as an amateur. I learned that if I donated my professional winnings to a charity I could regain my amateur status. All I had to do was to turn in my expense sheets and professional earnings to the Association, so I followed Benny's advice. More than anything, I still wanted to be top in my field.

Regaining my amateur status opened a new world for me. I traveled throughout New England and the eastern United States, playing in tournaments just about every weekend. I loved the travel and the competition, and I found my game improving. I had already learned from playing on the professional tour that my game improved when I competed with those who were better than I, but I also learned that I improved at an even greater pace when I played those at all levels. When players were better than I, it brought my game up; when players were at the same level, I worked on my mental game; and when players were of lesser caliber, I worked on my physical game. I gained confidence, loved traveling and exploring the eastern states, and enjoyed meeting all the new players. I even made some extra cash to help with expenses on the professional tour. I no longer had time to think about what was going to make my life fulfilling. I was too busy.

Chapter 11

Spring: 1984

Mental is as important as physical conditioning.

From September of 1983 through April of 1984 I won first place in eighteen straight women's open tournaments. Included in those wins were two New England regional championships, which qualified me for two Nationals. The more important of these two Nationals was the American Amateur Racquetball National Singles Tournament that was held in May in Houston. The top three finishers in this tournament would be placed on the United States Racquetball Team.

Was I ready for the Nationals? The experience of participating in so many competitions had allowed me to hone my mental game. Not only did I try out new strategies, but I also continued to study other players. I started to see which strategies and mindsets worked and which did not. At the same time, I was told numerous times "You're too nice on the court," and "You have to get mean," by people who cited examples to prove their point. Clearly, there were top professional tennis players who were so intense on the court that they threw tantrums and constantly argued with the referees; people suggested that I needed to be that intense in racquetball. I hated it when club members or friends told me this. I hated it so much that I became even more determined to prove that I could be a good sport, a friendly competitor, and still win. This became my next goal, and I used it to drive me to work even harder.

Paying attention to my own feelings, and those of my opponents, after winning or losing was my new area of study. I proved to myself that it was detrimental to feel too good about myself when I won, as if I were a better person because of winning. When I did this and carried my inflated ego into the next match, it was a distraction from playing my best. It created extra pressure to live up to an inflated ego, because if I lost that would mean I was less of a person. So I started to separate my feelings about myself from how I played. I knew I had total control over who I was, but not necessarily over whether I won or lost. No matter what the score I was determined to stay positive and fair, no matter what the circumstances. I was determined to be the best person I could be both on and off the court because, in the end, I had to live with myself.

I learned the importance of respecting every player regardless of how well they played. I knew anyone could beat me on any given day, so I took no one for granted and did not worry about how good my opponents were or how well they played. I realized I had no control over that; I only had control over what I did. If a player aced me in two straight games and won the match, I had nothing to be ashamed of or to feel down about. I could stay positive, study what my opponent did to win, and learn from the experience. This strategy helped cut down on distractions and allowed me to focus on my own game.

I also found that it was important to be aware of my emotional state prior to competitions. After much trial and error, I discovered that I played my best when

I was balanced between relaxation and excitement. If I was too relaxed, my reactions would be too slow. If I was too excited, I would hit the ball too hard and high, out of control. It was like finding room temperature on a thermostat. If I was too excited I needed to calm myself down by concentrating on each shot and by using relaxation techniques. If I was too calm I needed to get more excited by anticipating the challenge and the rewards of meeting this challenge. There was a certain medium point between calmness and excitement where I played at my peak. Once I had found the place on my emotional thermostat where I played my best, I would attempt to recreate it by closing my eyes and searching for the feeling. I did this before each match, as well as during the match between points and at time outs.

An added bonus to going to the Nationals was the fact that my brother Timmy and his wife Elaine had moved from Kansas to Wharton, Texas, about an hour south of Houston. It would be good to stay with them for the tournament and they were excited to have me. There was even a public racquetball court in Wharton where I could train. I made use of it the day I arrived.

The next day Elaine drove me up to Houston for my first match. The Houston YMCA, the host of the tournament, was the largest club I had ever seen. There were at least seventeen courts. More than eight hundred players were competing, and the draw sheets were huge. I had never been to such a huge tournament and I was nervous. Before my match I rode the stationary bike, ran sprints, and Elaine gave me a massage to help me relax. I then found a court where I could get my strokes into a groove, and afterward quieted myself in a corner, finding — through self reflection — that balanced state of emotions I knew I had to be in so I could play my best.

I won my first match, but Elaine was not satisfied. She thought I was too easy on the other player. We talked the full seventy-five minutes back to Wharton and I listened intently to what she had to say. Elaine did not say I had to get mean; she was saying I had to get more determined and needed to play with more will.

The next day, on the way up to the match, I reflected out loud and confessed to Elaine that I really did not like beating anyone, although I loved to win. I felt sorry for anyone I beat. Actually, I was just as surprised as Elaine to learn this about myself. It just surfaced during my talks with her. Elaine pointed out that it was important to play your best because it was better for your opponent. If you play your best they can learn from you; if you do not play your best it is like you are cheating them. I contemplated this and agreed that it was true. If someone did not play her best against me, I had a false sense of what I was up against and would not learn as much. So I worked on changing this unconscious mind set. I knew I would have to remind myself of this, as it was such a new concept that it would take some time to break my habitual thought patterns. I could feel a change in myself with this new realization. It felt like my will to win was freed.

The next match was the quarterfinals against the Junior National Champion. I kept the same warm up routine. I felt centered and ready to play, and I concentrated on keeping a strong determination through the whole match. I won in two games. Elaine felt I had improved in my determination, but she still thought I was not strong enough. She had me imagine that I was a jaguar ready to pounce on its prey. We worked on that imagery all the way back to Houston for my semi-finals match.

I was now playing for a position on the United States

National Team. I had never played my opponent and did not know her very well, but I did know she was from Hollywood, California, and I saw that she was a powerful left-hander. Her powerful swing did not bother me since my practice partners were generally hard-hitting men, but I lost the first game 21–16. I came back and was on a roll the second game and won 21–14. I walked out of the court for some water in between the second game and the tiebreaker. When I came back on the court I could feel that I lost the concentration I had in the second game. I lost 11–5 and, of course, disappointment swelled over me. I knew it was important to release my dissatisfaction over this loss, as it would seep into my body and affect my physical abilities. So I reviewed the positive things that had happened. I was happy to have made it this far in my first amateur Nationals and in my first tournament of this size. Plus I still had a shot at being on the team, as I would be playing for the third position on the US team as well as the third place finish in the tournament the next day. The realization of these facts allowed my spirit to rise once more. I kept them in mind as I started my preparation for the next day.

Elaine worked on my mental conditioning all the way home, and I felt a strong will and desire to win seep into my being. I was anxious to practice on the court; so off I went when we returned to Wharton and then again early the next day. I also received a massage; it was not a relaxing one, but one that awakened my body to prepare for the match. My goal this time was to maintain my mental edge throughout the entire match. I wanted to have my muscles relaxed but my mind pumped up at the same time. I wanted to be as willful and determined as a jaguar.

Again the match went to a tiebreaking game. This

time I remembered what I learned the day before and stayed in the court to keep my strokes and my mind in gear. It worked; I rolled to an 11-0 victory in the third game. I would represent my country at the World Championships in Sacramento, California.

I felt a peaceful bliss run through my body. I was thrilled that I had made the team, and felt delighted about all I had learned. I had experienced the fact that mental conditioning was as important as physical conditioning, and I was grateful to my sister–in–law for helping me to integrate the physical and the mental components that were essential to my game. I knew she had discovered more pieces to the victory puzzle and this discovery was as satisfying and as rewarding as the medal I was wearing around my neck.

Chapter 12

Summer: 1984

When the going gets tough, there are three choices: quit, do your best, or dig deep and play to the new level.

I would be flying out to Sacramento on July 11 for the World Championships. Once I settled in back home I suddenly realized this was only six weeks away. I had to get down to training immediately.

I heard there would be seven female players and seven male players coming to the World Championships from the United States. However, only five female and five male players would actually be competing in the tournament. The two National Doubles Champions would automatically be competing, but the remaining three slots would be filled by having a playoff among the five qualifiers when they arrived in Sacramento. Not only would I be competing against the top two finishers from the Nationals, but the winner of the Junior National Championship and the winner of the Intercollegiate National Championship would be competing as well.

I set my goal. I wanted to play in the World Championships, and definitely did not want to have flown all the way to Sacramento to be a spectator. I felt some pressure, but also felt my will kick in. I was determined, and trained consistently and aggressively for the next six weeks. While the club members were up in the restaurant listening to live music, eating, and drinking, I was in the court performing footwork drills and practicing my shots to get them into a groove, and I felt good about it.

I not only practiced my physical skills but my mental skills as well. At that time I was dating Tim, a young man I had met at the club, and he could tell I needed to work on concentration. To help he would play against me and be as aggravating as he could. That way I could train myself to concentrate on my game and not worry what other players, spectators, or referees were saying or doing. At least that is what he told me he was doing, but I think he enjoyed it as well. Initially Tim really did aggravate me, and I could tell it distracted me from playing my best. However, as time went on I was better able to block out his shenanigans and concentrate on my game. My physical game greatly improved because of it. This was one more example of the mind needing training just as much as the body. I was very appreciative of the workout he gave me, although I found it challenging.

Not only was my training schedule challenging, but life at work became challenging as well. One of the owners of the club called me, out of the blue, and asked me to come to his home so he could talk to me about something. I had no idea what it was about. I only knew he was recovering from gallbladder surgery at home so he could not meet me at the club.

I was totally shocked when I learned what he had to say. He charged me with stealing from the club. He said I stole from the pro shop and also stole time, meaning I was not working enough hours.

I was devastated by his accusations, and I stood speechless and shaking. I knew that, if anything, the club owed me for all the extra time I put in, and for running the pro shop. I had records to prove it, but he did not want to hear anything I had to say.

I went away feeling very dejected and still shaking with disbelief. I felt as if I had just been stabbed in the heart. I loved the club and the club members. Then I realized that it was not the club members who had said these things to me; it was one of the owners. I decided that, for the time being, I would continue working the way I had been, as I knew I had not done anything wrong.

I also called my best friends Joyce and Bob. They were like family to me and included me in every family celebration. When I told them about my conversation with the owner, they could not believe it either. After speaking with them, I decided I would talk with the other racquetball club in town, Manchester Court Club, to see if they were interested in having me work for them.

It turned out that, not only were they interested, but they had planned on speaking with me as well. After some negotiations a contract was drawn up, and it was agreed that I would start with them in the fall. I was really excited — but also sad. I felt as if the club members were my family and I was leaving them. However, many of them said they would follow me to Manchester Court Club and this lifted my spirits.

I had also been speaking with my parents. They had previously mentioned that they wanted to drive out to California in August to visit my sister, my one–year–old nephew, and my great aunt. They asked me if I would go with them to help with the driving. August is a very slow time in all racquetball clubs in New Hampshire with everyone enjoying the outdoors, so I told them I would go; and I told my club that I would no longer be working there after August 1st. I would be starting my new job on the first of September.

The management and the other two owners were very upset. They tried to change my mind but I would not budge. I was not going to work in an environment where I was not trusted.

Because of all my training I had developed plantar fasciitis and my heel was very painful to walk on. I had started physical therapy to help decrease the pain, but the pain would just not go away. At the same time my boyfriend and I were having troubles and not agreeing on our relationship.

So I was flying out to California — not on good terms with the club I loved, not on good terms with my boyfriend, and I was dealing with heel pain from plantar fasciitis. However, I was still determined to be one of the three women representing the US in the World Championships.

I arrived in Sacramento on July 11 and met the team at the club where the World Championships would be held. It was quiet in the club since the United States contingent was the first to arrive. The players would be housed in private homes, so the team met to decide who would stay where. When my coach, Ted, said that a sixty–year–old woman had volunteered her home for one player, I immediately jumped at the offer. I did not mind staying by myself; in fact, for this tournament and with everything going on in my life, I preferred it. Ted gave me a ride to the house. The next day we would all report to the club for the playoffs.

When I arrived at the home of my host family I was greeted by the owner, Diane, who showed me to a small cottage — next to the main residence — where I would be staying. My hostesses were Diane, her daughter Debbie, and Debbie's twelve-year-old daughter, Jenna.

I loved the little cottage. Although it was dark inside, it was very pleasant. It consisted of one room with a bed in the middle and a small bathroom in the back. I opened the refrigerator and there was an assortment of food and drink. My initial thought was that they must use this refrigerator for overflow from the house, but I soon found out that the food was for me. I was extremely grateful to have found myself in this little cottage, surrounded by such hospitality and warmth.

The cottage was just about a mile from the club, and the walk was not good for my heal pain, but it did feel good to have the independence of being able to come and go as I pleased. I arrived at the club early the next morning to prepare for the qualifying matches against my teammates. We would be playing a round robin; in other words I would be playing against the four other women to see who would be playing in the World Championship.

My first match was against the women's intercollegiate champion. I won in two games and felt good about how I had played. I then went on to lose my next two matches against the national runner up and the Junior National Champion, both by close margins in tiebreakers. I lost my fourth match against the National Champion, in two games. I felt very down. I knew it would take a miracle for me to be chosen to represent my country in the World Championships.

That miracle happened. As it turned out, there was a three-way tie for the third place as three of us had only won a single match. I won the third position on the team by having the most total points in the matches. When the coach announced the result, I could not believe it. All the training and work had not been in vain. I would be playing on the United States Racquetball Team in the World Championships!

Coach Ted wanted everyone to relax and rest after the grueling playoff schedule, so he graciously invited us to his vacation home on Lake Tahoe. The team drove up in two vans. On the way he wanted to stop at this hole in the wall restaurant called Cadillac Restaurant. He said the décor left something to be desired but the food was out of this world. He was right. I had some delicious barbecued ribs and enjoyed the camaraderie that was blossoming among the players. The junior champion, Loni, had unfortunately sprained her ankle in the playoffs. She and Katie would not be playing in the tournament, but they were supportive of my playing. I had a great time in Tahoe with the team, and appreciated the well-needed rest.

I woke up the next day with a very stiff back from all the games we had played. My heel was also very sore, but I was not going to let anything stop me. We drove the two hours back to Sacramento and, although I felt more rested, I was stiff and sore.

The team championship would begin the next day and would last three days. It is played in the same format as the Olympics. The countries are divided into two groups, or pools. All the players in one pool play each other with the top two teams in each pool advancing to the semi-finals.

We arrived in time to attend the opening dinner for all players competing in the World Championships. I was overwhelmed by what this dinner represented for me. I was in a room full of players with one thing in common, the love of racquetball. At the same time it was in a room full of people from around the world, from a myriad of cultures. I was curious about everyone there and wanted to meet as many players as I could. It dawned on me that they would need referees for the matches, so I decided to volunteer to referee as many matches as possible so I could see the different playing styles and meet the players.

Before the matches started, there were opening ceremonies in which we all marched with our teams and speeches were made. Then the tournament started. In the first rounds, I defeated players from Holland, Costa Rica, and Germany. They were not extremely tough matches and this gave me some time to heal and stretch. As a result, I was feeling better.

Our team won our bracket and then we went on to play against Canada for the gold medal. I suddenly realized I was not only playing for myself, but for my country. This thought, and the pressure I put on myself as a result of it, negatively affected my play. I could feel the stress building. I was playing against a tough opponent from Canada and lost the first game, then found myself losing 3–9 in the second game. I took a time out and reminded myself that I did not come here to play this way for my country. Mindy, the team captain, came over to the court after winning her match, and also gave me some tips. I then remembered the jaguar and I felt my determination rise; at the same time, the pressure I had put on myself seemed to dissipate. I never looked back. I came back and won that game and then the tiebreaker — securing an undefeated team victory over Canada. At the end of the day the US team went out for a celebratory dinner. I felt a great sense of relief in finding that I was able to come through for our team and be part of the victory.

The next day a rafting trip was scheduled for all the players to float down the American River. I loved the trip; it was relaxing and another great way to meet more competitors from around the world.

The following day was the individual championship. The format was single elimination, which meant that if you lost you were eliminated from the tournament but if you won you went on to the next round. I won my first round against an opponent from Holland. The next round was tougher as the player from Japan gave me a challenge, and my back was again giving me trouble. I won, but I could barely walk off the court after the match.

Since I was a referee at so many matches I had met many of the players from other countries. This turned out to be helpful when one of my new–found friends told a Belgian couple; Mivan and Sodil — who were chiropractors — that I was having back trouble. They came over and offered their services.

I had been to a chiropractor before, but Mivan was different. He said he used applied kinesiology, a method in which he tested to find the location of the weakness and gave an adjustment exactly where it was needed. I felt the difference at once and was stronger immediately after the adjustment.

I had also noticed something about my heel pain. It really hurt when I walked, but once I was on the court playing the pain seemed to go away. I assumed this had something to do with adrenalin and, perhaps, the fact that I was focused on the competition not my pain.

I was now in the quarterfinals playing the number one player from Canada, Crystal. I felt like things were going my way and, with this feeling supporting me, I was better able to focus my attention. Although Crystal and I were evenly matched, I won the first game 15–14, and then took the second game 15–8.

That evening I would be playing in the semifinals against Darci, that years' U.S. National Amateur Champion who had beaten me in the semifinals of that tournament. Darci had just come off a huge tournament in June, making it to the semifinals of the Women's Professional Nationals.

Prior to our match there was a different type of competition on the next court over. Players were using a radar gun to determine the speed of their shots. I decided to be tested. Everyone laughed when I walked onto the court because I had been labeled a soft touch hitter, not a power hitter. Darci had just hit the ball 104 miles per hour; my shot only registered 80, which brought on more laughter.

It honestly did not bother me. I did not care if they laughed. I knew if I could put the ball away at 80 miles per hour that was just as good as hitting it 104 miles per hour. I worked on staying focused. I knew I had lost to Darci three times that season, but they were always close matches. I felt the difference would be in my mental preparation, and I felt great mentally. I felt I was at my best, pumped up and ready to play well, but relaxed at the same time.

I came out and won the first game easily at 15–6, but Darci fought back and won the second 15–13. I remembered my lesson and stayed on the court for the tiebreaker. I could feel many thoughts and emotions wanting to creep into me, but I fought them off. I stepped out of myself and reflected. I could tell I needed to relax but stay pumped. My nerves were causing me to take large swings so, in between points, I concentrated on snapping my wrist quickly around. My self-reflection distracted me from any negative thoughts and, by working with what I learned through this reflection, I was able to stay focused.

The work paid off; I won the tiebreaker. The jinx was over. I could not believe it. I would be playing in the finals for the World Championship! The match was the following day against the top seed, Mindy, who was the current World Champion and my own team captain.

That night I had dinner with my hostess family. Debbie's boyfriend, Ron, came over and we had a wonderful meal. I especially loved getting away from the club and having a quiet distraction from all the excitement. They told me they would all come to watch me tomorrow.

After dinner I went back to my little cottage and attempted to put what was happening into perspective. I was so grateful to have made the team and to have the chance to compete — and I was especially grateful that I had won for my team and country. I was also excited about playing the next day and felt I was on a high that I wanted to hold on to.

The club and all my challenges back home seemed far away. I opened a card from one of the younger members of the club, Mike, a sixteen-year-old who often helped me with my racquetball drills, and decided to read it.

"You have done so much for the club and especially me and my family. I have heard many people say how much better you make our club than all the rest. It is really too bad you are unhappy here. You really deserve to win the tournament. Do it for yourself. You have given so much to everyone it seems you have neglected yourself. You have been training hard for this and you can do it. Everyone here at the club is behind you and really supports you. We all wish you the best of luck because you deserve it. Have a good time and remember think racquetball attitude. Love, Mike."

Emotions welled up inside me. The thoughtfulness of his writing and sending this card, as well as the thought that everyone was really behind me, filled me with emotion. I would try to win it for myself and for all those who supported me.

The next day Diane asked me if I wanted to see the backyard, which was filled with fruit trees. I said, "Sure." I toured the yard with Diane and felt as though I were walking through heaven. It was about one acre, and full of fruit trees and flower gardens. I felt the peacefulness of this environment flow through my blood and I held on to it. I knew I needed to keep the feeling of peace inside me. I would soon be playing the most important match of my life.

I headed off to the club. Mivan gave me a chiropractic adjustment by the pool, and I went in to warm up. I decided not to referee any matches that morning, but to spend the time preparing myself mentally and physically. As the time grew nearer, I could see the stands filling up. It turned out there were a couple hundred people packed in to watch the finals.

I saw that Diane, Debbie, Jenna, and Ron had spread themselves out so there would be cheering from all corners of the court. I saw Saul, the New England President of the American Amateur Racquetball Association, at the bottom corner of the glass back wall. He gave me thumbs up.

I knew that this would be a tough match. Mindy had more experience in international competition and knew how to be mentally tough. She had won the Nationals the previous year and was the current World Champion, having won the first ever World Championship.

My nerves worked against me the first game and I lost 15–9. Then I felt something in me that was hard to describe, but was similar to the feeling I had walking amongst the fruit trees that morning. I held on to that feeling. I became more consistent in my shots. I aced the serve a couple of times by hitting the crack where the front wall joined the floor, hits shots so that they passed Mindy by, and put balls away again and again. I won the second game 15–12, putting the match into a tie breaker. I again stayed on the court between games and worked at keeping the peaceful feeling. I also focused on keeping a quick and short snap of the wrist.

I was up 10–5 in a tiebreaker to 15 (sometimes tiebreakers are played to 11, but for this championship it was 15) and saw Saul in the corner holding up his hand and mouthing, "five more points." This made me buckle down to business. I scored again and looked back; he mouthed, "Four more points," with four fingers up. I felt his intensity and focus pierce through me and again hit a three–wall serve that died in the corner. Mindy called time out. I felt the momentum and remembered all the hard work I had put in up to this point. I again stayed in the court and in my zone. Time in. I looked back — three fingers up: Saul's intensity met mine. I served and quickly scored another point. Two fingers up — I felt the strength of determination; I served and passed the ball. One finger up. A long rally, and then I killed the final shot in a corner. Hands went up in the air, people yelled and cheered. I did it. I had won the World Championship with a score of 15 to 5!

Chapter 13

Summer–Fall–Winter: 1984

Expectation to achieve is constructive; pressure to achieve is destructive.

I slowly walked off the court, allowing the moment to sink in. I shook hands with Mindy and thanked the referee and line judges. My body felt weightless and I experienced a euphoria I had never known. I wanted to share this feeling with friends and family but it was so new to me that I actually just needed time to consciously sense the feeling and the moment. I was in a waking dream and very appreciative of all I was experiencing.

After a time, I gave in to the desire to speak with my parents and broke away and called them. Of course they were thrilled. But I did not know how thrilled they were until later, when we went on our planned road trip to California that August. Everywhere we stopped, whether it was a gas station, a restaurant, or a hotel, my father, with a gleam in his eyes, told everyone that his daughter (pointing to me) had just won the World Championship. I was somewhat embarrassed but did not mind; I was glad he was proud of me. I was careful not to let the win go to my head, knowing that I was not a better person for winning, just a very fortunate one.

After the tournament the whole team went out for

dinner, and a writer named Mitchell pulled me aside for an interview. I enjoyed the interview as he asked good questions, questions that allowed me to reflect on my past and the path I had taken to this point. He asked how I got started and also about my family. We talked about all that had led up to the tournament.

The interview helped me realize that this victory completed a puzzle I had been working on all of my life. I knew that my whole family, including my family of friends, had helped me with this puzzle. I knew that every loss, every win, everything I learned and worked on were important pieces of the puzzle. I realized that going to the University of Vermont, taking up racquetball, playing in a tournament in Montreal, meeting Perry, training in St. Louis, moving to California, struggling with injuries, and my jobs were all pieces of this puzzle. I realized that figuring out the physical and mental training elements were also big pieces. But more than anything, there was a feeling I had in this tournament that was different from anything I had ever experienced in any other tournament. I could not put it into words, but — more than the victory itself — I loved how I felt during the tournament. There was something that was carrying me through it — not in a physical, but in an emotional sense — that was helping me play at a higher level than my training alone could explain. This was the last, and most important, piece of this puzzle I had been searching for.

I became conscious of this almost immediately after my victory, but was distracted from really studying it because of another thought: Now I would have to prove that winning the tournament was not a fluke. Without understanding where this thought came from, I now focused my desire on proving I deserved the World Championship.

When I arrived home in Manchester Tim picked me up, and the first thing he said was "You will always be the 1984 Racquetball World Champion. No one can ever take that away from you no matter what." I appreciated that. It took pressure off, but at the same time I still held on to the feeling that I had to prove myself.

The club members were thrilled with my victory and it was nice to share it with them. I did more interviews with newspapers, radio, and even a couple of television stations did pieces on my victory. I was selected as the Manchester Union Leader's New Hampshire Athlete of the Month for July.

I also enjoyed the trip with my parents to California. It was great to take a break from all the hoopla. Then in September, I started my new job at the Manchester Court Club. The owners were a husband–wife team, Gus and Melinda, who were very down to earth. We became good friends and I felt relaxed, trusted, and appreciated. I wanted to work hard for them, and did.

I continued playing in the region and won three open tournaments in a row in Londonderry, N.H., Danbury, CT, and Yarmouth, MA. During this time my back once again began giving me trouble. On the way home from Yarmouth, it stiffened up so badly I had trouble getting out of my car, or even walking.

I decided it was time to go to the doctor. The doctor let me know the x-rays were negative but sent me to physical therapy. The physical therapy treatment included heat, ultrasound, massage, craniosacral therapy, and exercise. The combination worked to bring me back to playing shape in just a couple of weeks and I was ready to participate in the America's Regional Open in Quito, Ecuador, in early December.

I had to pay my way to Ecuador due to lack of sponsorship for the tournament, but, fortunately, my sister–in–law Elaine had cousins who lived there and she set me up to stay with them. This would save me hotel expenses, and it would be nice to get to know Elaine's cousins. The down side was that the rest of the team would be staying in a hotel and I would miss the camaraderie of being with the other players.

Everyone on the team met in Florida and we flew to Quito together. It was a rainy evening when we arrived. The first time we tried to land the pilot pulled up quickly and went around again to attempt another approach. It was a little scary so I was very happy and relieved when we were finally on the ground. I hadn't realized until we flew out on a clear day that the city was in the middle of a circle of mountains. Elaine's cousins met me at the airport and were very friendly. I felt comfortable with them at once.

I loved Quito. I took trips to the country with the team and to the city markets to get wonderful glimpses of life there. All the tournament players attended a bullfight together, and my cousins gave me an in–depth tour of Ecuador. Not only did I love Quito, but I also loved getting to know more of the racquetball players from different countries.

The racquetball club in Quito was small but beautiful. I noticed a different atmosphere there compared to the World Championships. The main reason for this was that it was a smaller tournament. Only teams from the Americas were invited. It was however, an important tournament since the winners would go to the World Games the next summer in London. I had already qualified for the World Games, as Mindy and I would automatically be attending based on our one–two finishes in the World Championships.

This did not mean that I did not want to prove myself in Quito. I did, but victory was not to be. I had a decent showing, winning ten matches, but losing to a Canadian player and ending up in fourth place overall. For me, it was not the finish that mattered as much as the realization that I did not feel I had played my best. I did not have that same feeling I had at the World Championships and that was bothering me. I wanted to find that feeling again, but did not know how to get it back. I felt as if something was blocking me.

Chapter 14

1985–1986

Self-reflection is the number one tool for self-growth.

I was determined to find the same zone I was in at the World Championships. I started reading books and listening to tapes about playing at your maximum potential, and I found they helped to keep me thinking in the right direction. I found that the key was really self-reflection. By reflecting on my play in a tournament or practice match through the use of videotape, I could pick out which thoughts and feelings were beneficial to my game and which were destructive. It was like weeding a garden; I wanted to destroy the negative thoughts and feelings — the weeds, and keep the beneficial feelings and thoughts — the harvest.

My first tournament in 1985 took place in Barre, Vermont, the first weekend in January. There were not enough players in the women's open so I played in the men's. I won my first round by defeating the club pro. My next match was against Ned, a seventeen year old who had made it to the quarterfinals of last year's Nationals and had won six junior regional titles. Ned and I had known each other since he was eight years old, and had played in Burlington when I was attending the University of Vermont. I had played Ned the past spring and had lost eleven to ten in the tiebreaker. Ned had really improved since then and soundly defeated me, but I learned an important lesson.

I could feel my self-confidence wane as it became clear that Ned was playing great. I knew that getting down on myself would not help my game and reasoned that if I challenged Ned, in my mind, to play the best he could, I would feel myself get pumped up and play at a higher level. I kept saying to myself, go ahead Ned, play harder, play your best. This blocked my fear of being totally outplayed and replaced it with determination and will. So, even though I lost the match, I liked the positive feeling I had and I hoped I could keep it all the time — whether I won or lost. I could see this new mental technique would help my game improve at a greater pace, by keeping the positive feeling all the time — no matter what the score, and no matter whether I won or lost. This was a real turning point, being able to thoroughly enjoy a match, and to have that wonderful feeling of accomplishment, even though the score did not indicate a victory.

I realized I would be better off redefining what winning was. I was determined to find a way to recreate the feeling I had at the World Championships — for that feeling alone would make me a winner. My victory would be to restore that feeling and to learn something in each match.

I spent the winter season working at the club and playing tournaments on the weekends. I experimented with different ways of staying focused on the court but still had not reached my goal. In the spring my back went into spasms again so I went to the physical therapy clinic. Peter, the physical therapist, worked with me and pointed out that my spine was very straight when it actually was supposed to have three curves: a lumbar inward curve, a thoracic outward curve, and a cervical inward curve. I told him that when I was in first or second grade my teachers had told me that good posture was standing up straight against the wall, so that is what I did. Peter emphatically told me that this was not correct. He told me that I had been compensating for this poor posture up until this point, but now my body was rebelling. He worked with me on my posture with stabilization exercises and craniosacral treatments. He also told me one more thing. He could see I was holding my musculature tight, and thought this was due to the psychological pressure I was putting on myself. He said I needed to relax, that I really was on top of the world in my life, and I needed to take some pressure off myself. All the pressure was hurting my body and mind.

I knew I needed to listen. I realized that my desire to prove to everyone that I was worthy of my World Championship was tightening me up. I worked to take that pressure off myself by constantly appreciating my abilities and what I had achieved. As a result I could feel my body relaxing. I began to understand that the competition was not between an opponent and I. It was between me and myself. I knew that negative feelings would occasionally creep in and hamper my ability to perform. I came to realize I had control over accepting or rejecting these feelings, and could stay in a positive frame of mind if wanted to. There was a competition between the negative and positive in my own mind, and I decided I was going to make sure I fed the positive.

This awareness made a huge difference in my focus on the court. I started to notice and categorize my feelings and thoughts as being constructive or destructive. I trained myself to reject the negative ones and replace them with positive ones. This led me to another discovery: If I hit a bad shot, I would close my eyes and picture myself hitting a good shot, a perfect shot. I practiced this mind control and, as a result, my game became more consistent. This mind control drill was working so well that I took it one step further. When I witnessed my opponent hitting a great shot, I would compliment him or her and would close my eyes and picture myself as the one who made the shot. In this way I learned from my opponents.

I loved this work. I could feel the positive energies well up inside me, and this translated into more consistent and improved play. In my self-reflection I came upon some of my innermost negative feelings, which I would never have discovered without this study. For example, it became palpably clear that, although I was taught to be nice and respectful, I was sometimes too nice. I needed to be more honest with myself and others. For example, in a tournament if the referee made a bad call against me it was better to respectfully protest the call than to just accept it. Protests of this sort were allowed in racquetball. By remaining silent failed to stand up for what I knew was correct, and lost self-respect. My work on standing up for myself, on not being too nice, increased my self-confidence. This self-confidence sent messages of strength to my mind, which translated into better play.

As I continued this work, I found that it was just as important to be honest and to correct referees when they missed calls that were in my favor. This was important for two reasons. Not correcting these calls when I knew they were wrong caused me to feel guilty. They gave me the possibility of winning a match I did not really deserve to win. Being honest benefited me by increasing my self-respect.

There were many other emotions I found destructive. I overcame jealousy by appreciating all that was good in my life. I overcame negative judgments with tolerance and understanding, insecurity with emphasis on my positive qualities, anxiety with calming, overconfidence by seeing the positive qualities in my opponents, impatience with patience, and as other negative emotions arose I took care of them in similar ways.

I was now ready to reflect back to the World Championships to try and determine why I had played at my peak. While playing in the World Championships I was having heel and back problems, so I did not feel I was physically at my peak. It was not that I was in top physical shape. I was not. I remembered the loving excitement I experienced in the tournament through participating with players from around the world. Then there was the appreciation I had felt for my host family who took me into their home and treated me with such warmth; the feelings I had when I read the card from Mike at the club, and how supported I felt by the club members who cheered me on from New Hampshire.

Now I was on a roll. I could feel I was getting closer. One day during this time I was playing a practice match, and I went to the front wall to gather the ball after a rally. All of a sudden I felt a warmth in my chest and diaphragm. It felt so good. This was the same feeling I had when I was walking in the yard with my host family in Sacramento, amongst the fruit trees. That peaceful and loving feeling had returned. It was like I was being guided. I was in a flow where nothing was good or bad. Everything just was, and it was right. I knew this was the zone I had been searching for, and I wanted to hold on to it. I continued playing the match, just holding on to that feeling. I did not care or remember if I won the game, I only cared that the feeling returned. I wanted to bottle it up and keep it forever.

I tried my best to keep this feeling for every match, but I would lose it through lack of concentration, or by focusing on negative events. Sometimes the distractions were uncontrollable, like having to deal with injuries or an inconvenient travel schedule prior to a tournament, or reacting to a bad relationship. Sometimes I would lose it because of internal events: my competitive spirit would rise and I would be overcome with a desire to win, or my pride would surface with a fear of losing and shaming myself, or all sorts of different negative feelings would appear before me.

Through self-reflection I was able to catch these negative emotions and would use my mental strategies and mind control to rid myself of them so they wouldn't block me from the loving flow. I filled myself up with appreciation for my life and all the gifts that had been bestowed on me, including the fact that I had rediscovered the zone. This appreciation and gratitude helped to prevent negative emotions from arising.

I discovered that my negative emotions and thoughts had been blocks obstructing me from returning to playing at my peak. It took me over a year of study before it came to me. But once it did I was able to find the zone over and over again as I competed in New England tournaments and on the professional tour. Regaining this feeling did not mean I always scored more points than my opponent, but to me it meant I won because I knew I was playing at my best and I could not ask for better than that.

Chapter 15

Spring 1986 – spring 1990

From the greatest challenges come the greatest rewards.

As it turned out I did find — more often than not — that I would come out ahead in points when I was in the zone. I won regional tournaments, again rose in the professional rankings to the top twenty, and won another national title, the thirty–five and older tournament. I was also privileged to be appointed assistant coach to the United States Racquetball Team in 1987, joining the team to participate in the Pan American games in Colorado Springs, Colorado, then traveling to Santa Cruz, Bolivia, for the America's Regional Tournament. In 1988, I helped to coach the team to another World Championship in Hamburg, Germany.

A thought came to me while in Houston attending the 1986 Nationals. It was that I was now over 30 and single, and I needed to think about the future. I was going to have to take care of myself and I wondered if I needed to expand my life options beyond racquetball. I found myself sitting in the bleachers in Houston brainstorming with my New England racquetball friends about what I was going to do with my life.

One of the beautiful benefits of racquetball competition was the friendships I developed. I loved the sport

...use the majority of the players left the competition on the court. Off the court — the relationships were separate; no one was better or worse for having won or lost. These were the best kind of friends: ones with whom I could compete against in mutual respect, and then be trusting companions off the court.

My New England racquetball friends were most definitely this way. They lightheartedly attempted to find me some vocation that would take me as far from New England as possible, jesting that they would have a better chance at winning with me gone. One of them asked, "How about becoming a physical therapist?" I tried that idea on. I quickly realized that physical therapy fit me very well. I had previously considered the profession because my physical therapist back home had recommended it to me, and because I had really enjoyed kinesiology in school. The more I thought about it, the more excited I became. I decided I would try to get into physical therapy school. When they heard this my New England friends quickly suggested I find a school out in California, kiddingly recommending that I go as far from New England as possible.

When I arrived back in New Hampshire I asked myself again: Was this really what I should do? I could sense that it was. Thinking about physical therapy school brought back memories of when I ended up at the University of Vermont by the seemingly chance suggestion of my headmaster. It brought back feelings of how I got into racquetball through a college course. It brought back the memories of how I found jobs in St. Louis and New Hampshire, seeming by accident. The feelings I had when I thought about studying physical therapy were the same as in all these cases. I knew it was the right decision.

Just as all of the other events had flowed easily, so did getting into physical therapy school. I looked over the requirements and it appeared that since I already had a B.S. in physical education I only needed to take a year of chemistry to qualify for admission. If I was accepted, I could then transfer in as a sophomore at a physical therapy school. I had been out of school for ten years and knew it would be a challenge to return. I decided I would try an experiment. I wanted to see if I could use what I had learned in racquetball to become a successful student. I decided I would undertake my studies like I was preparing for a tournament. I intended to learn all I could, stay positive, and love what I learned. I returned to school and started my experiment. Soon, I could feel it was working and I successfully passed both semesters of chemistry with high marks.

I applied to two physical therapy schools. The day that I heard that University of New England (UNE) had accepted me into the second year of their program was one of the happiest days of my life.

I had heard that UNE had a tough program and I knew how challenging it would be for me. When I was in grade school, my parents worried that I was not smart enough to pass the entrance exam to get into John Burroughs High School, the private high school they wanted me to attend. I did pass the exam and attended Burroughs with grades of B's and C's. As a physical education major at the University of Vermont I had a B average, but there was a big difference between a physical education major and physical therapy courses.

I decided the best chance I had was to continue my experiment and use all the strategies I used in racquetball. My intention was to learn as much as I could for my

...are patients' benefit so I could assist them as much as possible once I became a physical therapist. I worked hard, but attempted to stay relaxed. I kept my body in shape by working out and by playing a few tournaments. I studied every moment when I wasn't sleeping or working out. When there was a test or a practicum, I put myself in tournament mode by remembering the feeling I had when I was in the zone. There were many stressful times and many new negative emotions to confront, but I used the same strategies I had developed in racquetball to release them. I let them go and trained myself to stay positive and to appreciate the opportunity I was given. Due to this attitude, creative powers rose within me. Out of them came the idea to tape my classes as I took notes, to use the tapes to make sure I had complete notes, and then to change my notes into question and answer tapes from which to study. I used these question and answer tapes to study when I was driving, working out, or doing any task in which I could listen to the tapes and perform the activity at the same time.

This approach worked so well that, to my surprise, I graduated with highest honors. I knew without a doubt this was due to using the strategies, skills, and attitudes I had learned as a competitor. I was also given an honor I never expected. I did not know why but, to my surprise, I was elected by my class to be the class graduation speaker. Of course I accepted.

In preparation for the speech, I knew I needed to prepare in three ways: I needed to work hard, I needed to have a positive focus, and I had to be in the zone. When I was in the zone ideas would flow into me. I knew this through experience. I knew if I kept away negative emotions that blocked the pathway, and if I discarded and cleared myself of negative thoughts, I would be able to connect with some source that transcended my own intelligence. I knew that was what happened at the World Championships. I had no doubt that I had assistance in winning from this source. When looking back over my life, I started to recognize all the times when I realized I had been guided. I found a strong desire deep inside of me to live for these times. I felt like a kid starving for fantasy and magic. But this was different; this was real. It felt more real than life itself.

The idea for the graduation speech came to me from this same source. I would speak about our human tendency to blame tension and stress on everyone and everything but oneself. I saw this constantly while I was in school. The fault always lay with school, homework, or tests, never with oneself. I was grateful that this idea came to me and attempted to maintain the inspiration while writing the speech. Since I had so little experience writing speeches and had poor English grades in school, I was aware that I would only do my best if I could keep this channel of inspiration open.

Graduation day came. When I was called to speak I took a deep breath and walked up to the podium. To me this was as challenging as playing in the World Championships. I found myself walking into the gymnasium, packed with over 1,000 people including Senator George Mitchell who was the guest speaker. I kept fighting off the negative nervous thoughts that threatened to paralyze my body. I focused on what I was going to say. I knew I had worked hard and had memorized my speech. I believed in what I was going to say. Now it was important to let go of all thoughts so the speech could flow from my heart.

On Mother's Day 1990 I began my speech to the

graduating class of the University of New England in Biddeford, Maine:

So... we've almost made it. Our last challenge, prior to being an official graduate, is being able to walk up to receive our diploma. It appears to be an easy task, but there is always that chance of tripping on our own robe or the steps and falling in front of over 1000 people. Think about it. . . . Does that thought in any way make you nervous? If it does then it is an example of how you can take any task you want and make it stressful on yourself; it is your choice. Although I was the one who suggested the possibility of tripping, those who became nervous chose to accept my thoughts and those who stayed cool and calm rejected my thoughts. Throughout our years here it seems it's been easy to blame our tension on everything and everyone else except ourselves; school, homework, tests, presentations. Are they really the cause of our tension? Or is the cause of stress within us?

I have an example I'd like you to consider: A leading psychologist ran a study. He placed a two-foot by twenty-foot plank on the floor. He then placed a hundred dollar bill at the end of the plank and stated to a fourteen-year-old boy that if he could walk across the plank he could have the hundred-dollar bill placed at the end. The boy accepted and quickly crossed the plank. The doctor then put three hundred dollars at the end of the plank and gave the boy the same challenge. Again the boy accepted and decided to show off by hopping on one foot backwards to collect the money. The doctor then put five hundred dollars at the end of the plank, but placed the plank between two skyscrapers twenty stories tall. He gave the boy the same instructions. The boy attempted, but his knees were shaking and muscles were so tight he could not move. What was the difference? The plank was the same one that he walked backwards on with one foot. The difference in the ability to perform was all mental. The boy's concentration on the fear of failure caused his physical abilities to diminish. Our mental attitude going into presentations, or taking exams, very often dictates our performance just as the boy's attitude dictated his performance. The psychologist then polled a number of mothers. Would they cross the plank if it was to save one of their children? Most agreed they would, because their concentration would only be on their child. But one mother thought and then replied with a smile, 'That, Doctor, depends on which of my children is to be saved.'

How has our attitude been these last few years? Have we been stressed? Is school to blame, or is it our fear of failure, or is it the pressure <u>we</u> put on <u>ourselves</u> to receive a high grade. Should we decrease our stress by decreasing our risk taking? Or by working on our own mental attitude? If we understand that we have control over our attitude and that our tension stems from within, then we should not be afraid to take on any risk, whether it is to take on a new job, run for senator, or work toward world peace. . . .

As soon as I had finished a wonderful feeling of relief

flowed through me. I walked down the steps and was greeted by a standing ovation. My teachers and fellow students shook my hands and hugged me. I felt the same feelings I had following the World Championships. I could tell that this was due to the process I put into place leading up to the speech. The same process I had found through racquetball had put me in the peak performance zone: passion for what I was doing, a positive mental attitude, a healthy body, and an openness to a communication that guided me and allowed me to do better than if I attempted to prepare out of my own physical abilities.

Now that I made it through graduation and had been successful in my goal of assimilating all I had learned in racquetball into becoming a physical therapist, my new goal would be to integrate all that I had learned into my daily life. I would attempt to integrate these methods into my relationships, my job, and into day–to–day routines. I would attempt to live in a peak–performance state. I knew how important it was to ward off negative thoughts and feelings, both those coming from inside, and those from outside. Harboring negative thoughts seemed to block me from attaining that state in which I performed at my best. They blocked the wonderful feeling of elation, peace, and fulfillment that came from being in the zone. Having experienced what happens when I achieved that ideal state motivated me to build habits of positive living.

I found that racquetball competition was a wonderful venue in which to grow and find my best self. Through sports, music, dance, drama, education, and, probably in every endeavor of life, one has the opportunity to work to achieve one's own peak performance state.

I realized that my process in racquetball was a microcosm of how I needed to live my life. The habits I formed in this simple arena enabled me to find how to be my best. How I would integrate all of these lessons into my life was my next challenge.

Eventually I learned that, in my day to day living, I should reverse the process I went through in racquetball. My initial emphasis in racquetball had been on the physical aspects of the sport. I worked on being in the best possible shape — hoping that was the answer, but I found that physical skills were not enough. I then started using my mind, thinking of strategies to make me a better player; strategies like working on one skill at a time until it became habit, then thinking only positive thoughts, then closing my eyes and feeling that every shot was perfect. These strategies helped, but they were not the full answer. Then at the World Championships I felt something new deep inside me — a deep love, appreciation, and peace culminating in a knowledge that everything was as it should be. Holding onto that state, the synchrony of my mind, body, and soul, resulted in my ability to play at a higher level than I had ever experienced. So it seems that the answer to performing at ones best is to reverse of the process I went through in racquetball. The first priority is to find that emotional state of passion and love from inside yourself, then develop a positive mental attitude, and then out of this loving positive state, train your body to perform.

My dream is for more people to experience this wonderful feeling and find the answer for themselves. Eventually there will be more people living out of their best, knowing that every being is an intrinsic part of all there is, with every person being unique and important in this whole.

From racquetball I learned that all changes start with

my own self. What a great challenge it is to weave these lessons from sports into my day-to-day life. I have gained the knowledge that when the greatest challenges arise, the challenges that appear great than my own human intelligence, there is always this process, and this source, that I can look to, to find THE ANSWER.

CPSIA information can be obtained
at www.ICGtesting.com
Printed in the USA
FFOW01n1015250915
17203FF

9 780982 271513